FIRST PRINTING
of which this is Number

350

THE SORROWS OF COLD STONE

Poems 1940–1950

Certain of these poems first appeared in:

Accent

A Little Treasury of American Poetry

American Thought, 1947

Foreground

Harper's

Harper's Bazaar

Mademoiselle

Origenes (Havana)

Poetry: A Magazine of Verse

The New Yorker

The Sewanee Review

The Tiger's Eye

THE

Sorrows

of

Cold Stone

POEMS 1940 & 1950

John
MALCOLM
BRINNIN

DODD MEAD

The following poems are reprinted from NO ARCH, NO TRIUMPH by John Malcolm Brinnin, by permission of Alfred A. Knopf, Inc. Copyright, 1945, by Alfred A. Knopf, Inc. LOVE IN PARTICULAR, A RIVER, SHAPES IN SHALLOW WATERS, FOR MY PUPILS IN THE WAR YEARS and VIEWS OF THE FAVORITE COLLEGES.

The following poems are reprinted from THE GARDEN IS POLITICAL by John Malcolm Brinnin, by permission of The Macmillan Company. Copyright, 1942, by John Malcolm Brinnin. A LETTER, ROWING IN LINCOLN PARK, EVERY EARTHLY CREATURE, THE LATE SUMMER and AT THE AIRPORT.

Drawings by courtesy of the Betty Parsons Gallery, New York City.

PRINTED IN THE UNITED STATES OF AMERICA

these poems are for
B. R.

Contents

THE

WIND

IS

ILL

Stamos '47

The Double Crucifixion

Death hunted me for life, wherefore
Transported otherwise, I died before.
   The agony was waiting among stone,
   Uncertain, threatened, left alone
To entertain, in sight of torches, love
The cup that will not pass, love the lost chance;
     Denied love more than once,
I kissed the rod that smote, the hand that gave,
And thought: what chooses me I choose;
The shadow of undoing knows
Not circumstances nor identities.

So set to have what would have me,
I watched the hangman prune the anguished tree
   And fashion, like attendant fate,
   The face I printed on a borrowed sheet,
The branch I shouldered, the prize thorn I shed.
His lance was ready long before the thrust
     Discharged my pent-up lust;
His lucky bones, before my bones were laid,
Dismantled me. Still would I turn,
Burning to be so fixed again,
Consumed by the event I cannot mourn.

Spread-eagled, sticks and stones, I lay
And kissed the flesh that matched flesh under me;

In double crucifixion at arms' length
We crossed the threshold of our doubled strength,
Drank darkness in, and drunk with double night,
Were sheathed, unsheathed with lightning, sweet swift
      sword
      Uplifted, sweet, swart God,
Sustain me this soft outrage in your sight.
When, love, your tender hands undid
My body from your body, the dead
Landscape of heaven filled my sleeping head.

Cradle Song

Who is my shepherd, that I shall not want?
Who with earth-roughened hands
Will loose the spike that joins my ankle-bones,
And bear me home, and have me in his house?

I seek a father who most need a son,
Yet have no voice to call
One or the other, nor wind nor oracle
To publish me, where I am meant to die.

Who is my uncle, that shall intervene,
Assist the turning wheel
That like the running towers of the sun
Will smash my king's house and my cockleshell?

Who is my mother, that shall make my bed?
Who with gold-beaten rings
Shall quicken me, that I beget my son
Where my cold father with his lust lay down?

Who is one blind, that has already seen
Blood where it shall fall soon?
He knows my ways and how I rule this ground.
In his perpetual light I would be found.

The day is in the sea, the night grows cold.
Is the event long past?
The suckling beast knows where I lie alone.
I seek a father who most need a son.

The Wind Is Ill

All's ill and will be so
Until what will not wed is brought to bed
Charged with a savior's brief
For coupling conscience with black flesh and blood;
Until the arch supports its crushing roof
And eggs in nests of snow
Tame the long undertow
With clattering allelulias from the shell
All's well so charily
The tongues of iron bells will fail to tell
A wiser homily than verily,
Say lack, say touch and go.

All hail wind-cocks that shift
The livelong architecture of hot sand
From leaf-pocked flesh to stone;
Where blunt-nosed marbles, dying in the wind,
Drift grain by grain toward covered Babylon,
East comes soft, west comes swift,
Until of all that's left
The lights of time patrol, yet cannot tell
All ails so bitterly
The marathon bird is buried where it fell,
And banished utterly
The little dog that laughed.

All hell pursues the pair
Who first touched fruits of flesh to find them sweet
And sadly separate;
The hunt is hot and what is chaste is caught,
Stripped of its leaf and tangled in a sheet
While the bored glories sit
Before and after it,
Clocking the chores of ecstasy untouched.
Ah, well, the wind is ill
And if such sails as loom are seldom beached,
Farewell's the most of hail,
Here, there, and everywhere.

Fêtes, Fates

O not to bless my soul
Come kinsmen wrist, thigh, lip and all their creatures,
Guests of my board and bed,
Companions of intolerable pleasure,
Whiplashing tongue, taut ankle, swiveled head
Who by blood's stream and vessel
Make picnic of my will,
Eating its music with an insect measure,
Unraveling its laws
Piecemeal until, in the disgrace of nature,
Whim is my wantonness
And wit's my jack-of-all.

Their host and cage long since,
I am death's head above them where they take
The welcome of my house,
Yet cannot be blindstruck, nor turn my back
When all my flying fragments kiss and toss
Sense to its blunted sense,
Love on its dear love's clowns.
To mend me, mind me, bind me where I break—
Heart's blood, mind's rift of light—
Is all my will; all, all, my lack:
Those meshings make my fate,
Those hungers call my dance.

Goodnight, when the door swings
And the great lock's shuttle tooth comes down
On darkness and hail fellow,
Goodnight, my smile, insatiate eye, bald frown,
Goodnight. In colder carnivals we'll follow
Our one pleasaunce among
A quietude, ere long,
That will our disparateness so bundle down
In earthen intimacy,
My ways and will and yours will move as one
When guest by host shall lie
Lengthwise, and right by wrong.

Faces, Faces

I leave for an expanse
Unpainted with the manlike face of God
Where free among free forms
The mast-and-spar, the gate and thunderhead,
The cabbage, wolf's-jaw, and the sere Christ-thorn
Across my blind foresight
Move like a field of light;
I follow shadows towering from spilled shades
That from the first, all ghost,
Charged with a dark my dearest neighborhoods;
At last, so self-possessed
I range their dread terrains.

As in the voice of wind
The locked jaws of the silent sing through bones,
The face of nothingness
Enchants and haunts the face of man God wants
To mask Allhallows with boys' mysteries;
As time eats time like sand
Nets of a world's wind bind
The death's-head moth, the lilac and the clock;
The air's face God's face marries,
Spawning new martyrs on the bridal rack
From which the child of space is
Lifted in blood and burned.

Have left and leave now ever
Sleeping head on elbow-cradled arm
To meet the window-face,
The foundling brainstone, the benign glowworm
And, far from houses, the fog-featured rose;
Down, down like diver
In his blue free-swimming fever
I kiss the fathering faces of us all
Which, for they are not flesh,
Appear and fade like figures on a shell
The far flung rains shall wash
And winds shall topple over.

Before There Was No Reason in the World

Before there was no reason in the world
As now there is
I was the bough bent easy by a bird
I was the vague blue-grazing flock
The sleeping and invisible

Before there was no reason in the world
As now there is
The course of waters was my only course
My repetitions oceans' sough and swell
My seasons pleasurable

Before there was no reason in the world
As now there is
To measure time from sleep I rose to sleep
To measure space I pastured on surprise
O meadows of resemblances

Before there was no reason in the world
As now there is
I was the grove on whose mosaic floors
The seeds of otherwise were spent
My gods had many arms

I was the Caesar of unmarshalled grass
Faustus in the branches
My first ambitions were my sorrows long
Before there was no reason in the world
As now there is

At Land's End

I

On the windy ranches of the water-rat
Nine stiff wind-scoured ribs
Upright in music.

II

So was the Ark a-waste on a plateau:
Processional giraffe, lynx, ocelot
Printing the sand below.

III

A house to stave off life,
An avenue of never-arching elms.

IV

What came here burning from the land
Like a tower running
On the times of sand?

V

I was so trundled nine months in a wave,
Set down in blood on a sad shore,
My fingers—roots,
My hair, downgrowing grass.

VI

Polyborus Chimango, Darwin said,
Sits in the ribs of cow or horse
Like a bird in a white cage.

VII

Its three lashed crosses bare,
A Yankee Clipper like a floating Calvary
Ground to resurrection here.

VIII

See how the gulls, those protestants,
Confer like merchants in the organ-haunted chambers
Of cathedral bones.

IX

A great egg hatched within a cloud,
Its silken panels opened like a wall?
No.
The beauty of this dying lies
In its last verticals.

X

A basket of arrivals and departures.

XI

What do these ribs ache for—
Heart's blood? Mind's eye?
Pride of immortal soul?

XII

What do they cradle?
Love?
Time?
Air?

XIII

Air.

Father, Son, and Holy Ghost

God The Father:
Cock-o'-the-shell in panelled Paradise
Still bubble-easy, my good nature was
Chickadees in apple trees, the burst
Cacao and potato-fat strawberry,
The snow-lashed edelweiss and poking cherry—
Plain fare of heaven spilled to such excess
The morning glory antlered everything
In sight. And where the lean iatric herb
Obtained, what was its use in that sweet grass?

God The Son:
As I am of Thee, and as from Thee speak,
No use, and as Thine echo, of no use.
O what a lie I fell for all for this!
Forgive me, Father, your ripe fantasies.
The ship-shaped shadow spoiling on the hill
Has me in mind and would have me in tow.
Come down, blunt burden, bear me well below,
Ride me to earth as I ride over you.
O flesh I rub against a splintered tree.
God fearing spirits wanting grace to die
Will feed thee upward, and downward will feed thee.

God The Holy Ghost:
The seed divided and the shivered glass
Assemble into and resemble one;
Shapes of new accidental mornings pass
Where God The Father hangs with God The Son.

The Maze

Unless to enter—
   Beast of the red cave
With unfixed eye,
   Love has no thread to leave
Nor post to guide
   What it would save—
By love's unravelling to begin,
The woven space grows whole again.

So to withdraw
   From the city of God
Love's amplitude,
   The mind's five-barred
Threshold, salt-cragged
   Box of wood—
To found the water-locked sea tower
In the footprint of the Minotaur.

To have loved one
   Gathering hand,
Flesh, idea
   And intellectual wind
Is to be sown
   On barren ground—
Cold harvest, burn with such hot light
Will strike the taller him who sheds it!

Song for Doomsday Minus One

Self-cast from shell and cave,
God's genius and his whip-lashed reptiles have
Quit the slow shape of birth
For the fine fission and cloudbank of death;
On God's cold eye the coin is placed,
On shine of wheat the shade of rust;
By bating of a breath
The torse of flame in the full-bodied boughs
Falls ashen from the ashen tree
That, evergreen, drew rivers from their source
And ransomed the black seed of mystery.
O round world crowned with snow,
Fear Man, and fear His embryo.

Over the green land watching
Infant turnings, blood-red eye and wing,
The speckled softness and
Soft plungings of fern-roots, fern-folded hands,
The mothering grace of earth and sun
By fiat of self-love shines on;
Over the dark compound
And golden seam, lullay, the mild hands turn;
Over the mounds of burial,
Lullay, the wheeling zodiac, dead-watching, burns,
And in the space between four seasons fall.
O green world where you go,
Fear Man, and fear His embryo.

In cloth of sleep long curled,
Vine into vein across the underworld
　　Of fire that speaks to ice,
The waking man knows first his nakedness;
　　Though in the valence of his will
　　God and his reptile twin lie still,
　　　His web of conscience is
The egg of fable on slow-burning sand
　　That keeps, before the scorched age comes,
Blood cradled well and long song of the mind,
The fluted bones and music of the tombs.
　　O turning world ground slow,
　　Fear Man, and fear His embryo.

　　As leaf-taking May, leavetaking,
In the soft pursuit of summertime, takes wing,
　　The God's-breath egg of doom,
Like the shadow of the moon on time to come,
　　Falls on time out of mind and time
　　In whose bleak reaches shine the dim
　　　Lights of millennium.
Though blood that fuses what it must refuse
　　Labor the womb and dragging bough,
Love the old wind on which the black seed flies
Saves for a time the fiction of time's flow.
　　World of that overblow,
　　Fear Man, and fear His embryo.

Shapes in the Shallow Waters

Spending his whole experience of space
With handsome fallacy, the burning boy
Swan-dives toward his marine metropolis
And in the plumage of blue water-smoke
Makes boiling colors all his languages.

How laughable the hiss of this sea-death:
The fine blonde energy so spluttered out,
Its arc no matter more than a tossed match
Or a comet swallowed over conversation.
How thin the sheetings of this marriage-bed.

Since lack and love sing only at their crisis,
His music falls forwards and afterwards;
See how the diver is himself dissolved
Where irises on the dilating pool
Drop one free-floating feather for a child!

Is talk of weddings, then, but talk of death,
And every day but where he dies again?
His crystal city a submergéd hope
Half water-light, half memory? The sea
Drags under what it cannot free.

So in a wink a flying hand farewells
A decade's love or love for twenty minutes
With the same flame. How now these whispering shells
And rocking skulls forever souvenir
The first and ultimate waters of it all.

The shifty limpet on his rocky shore
Contrives a conch to make life possible,
And the unbelievable giraffe achieves
A dainty salad from the lissom tree;
Pretending he is flora in a pond,
A silly fish will emulate a frond
To trick the appetite that savors him;
A rabbit in the snow will do the same.

Like tinted views from a dismantled fair,
These illustrations fail, being outworn;
Who would construct a summerhouse or myth
To shade him from the elements of love
Is naked of resource; for when like fate
Love holds to nature unregenerate
On calendars that page the names of time,
The newest grief retells the oldest theme.

Since war, the matter of a generation,
Blunts as it must the savior and the fool,
Fathers and sons in terror worlds apart
Communicate in silence and mute signs;
The accurate bombs that scatter sanity,
The child of Guernica who cannot see
That innocence is death, acquaint me now;
I have learned armor I would disavow.

What grace survives the city's glass and stone,
What facet points the cosmopolitan?
To eke a diamond from its mineral floor
Earth rakes its faculty for quake and tide;
Yet in the city's blaze the millions go
From crib to crypt, nor any gem to show.
Ah, there the heart of man knows less itself
Than the least pink shell upon a watery shelf.

Like feathers on a swan, indifference coats
The reptile remnant of our primacy;
Debauched of tongue in time's slow sabotage,
Both tragedy and outrage come to ash;
Then is the heart adaptable to death,
As creatures who employ the earth, and breathe
The vivid air, ascend, superior;
Who comes to his instruction, stays to fear.

The sun of Genesis is shining still,
Though God is shifted to his place in time;
May evil, here, pace like the captured leopard
While love contends dynastically with love;
May earth in its success provide for all
Who lack the logic of the sorry snail,
Who die without a candle, or remain
To citizen the natural state of man.

The Gospel of John

In the word—(arch voicelessness of God
Trolling the void for God His Infancy,
Calling the simmering waters sane, wherein
The architecture of its accidents
Hangs in the chant and gong of foamings down
To hunger's hugest in the spawning dark
Sea-valleys of the flesh; and down, down, down
Angels, cherries and red princes falling
In cars archaic, chariots of flame,
Or by some indolence of parachutes
Upslowed through heaven's salient and gate,
Their wreaths in ash, their heads like planets still,
Their eyes in meditation upon ebony,
Downward sliding as the spider slides on black
Telegraphy, twitching its vehemence,
Splitting the apple from the bough whereby
All ransoms are made possible—the seed,
The dance, the kiss and fin of every shape
That waits, like a breathing fern, on the sills of night
And breathes the darkness in)—was the beginning.

THE

WORM

IN

THE

WHIRLING

CROSS

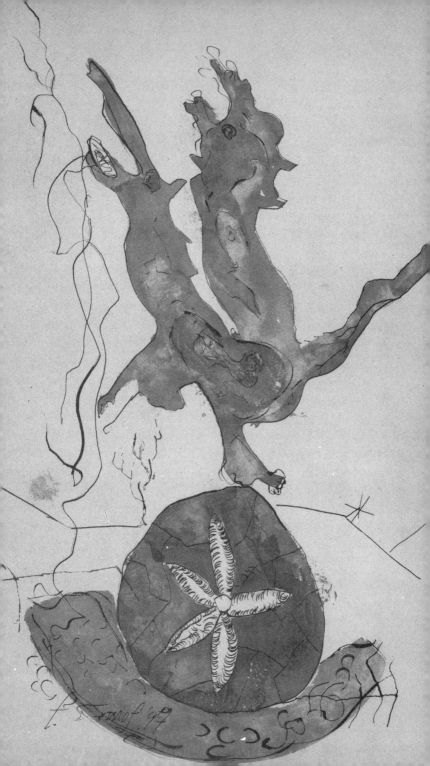

The Worm in the Whirling Cross

No further, fathering logos, withering son,
Shall I my sense for want of grace confess,
But vouch this matter of decaying green
That with a shark's tooth grin
Hinges the rooftree of my dwelling place.
Anguish I caught when I walked apple-wise
Shows me forever the first sun I mourn:
Wild Tigris at full spring, giraffes and O,
That water-logged, fell swoop of genesis.
What excellent ray divines it now? to learn
How leaf's mould burns, I would cross grain with you.
When your all-hallowed dome's dove-tailing brows
Fall to, by inscape clearing manscape new
My groundswelled pride shall greet hailstorm and stress.

I'd east, I'd west, O dark idea of sleep
If from this long idlesse and chrysalis
You'd spread your birdwise fan of shut third eyes
And on the cryptic idioms of snow
And tumid greensward show
The idols of your night to my idyllic day.
O toward identity
Be witness angel and dark partisan.

Upthrust down trodden bedrock's mighty main,
My slow bones stretched on tide-ledge, bog, and dune;

Time's tanglefoot, blood's vein that gags and blinds
Twin to his hungry intertwining twin,
I brushed big fish and fisted my curled hands
At brute Tyrannosaurus and tit-wren,
Honing the spirit flesh would eat alive,
Until, touched with the phosphor of self-love,
The forebrain glowed and light knew it was light.
Around that influence the flying fox,
Flanked by the archaeopteryx,
Sailed through the gloom, and restless under it
The little eohippus cropped his field;
One weather told the world how it grew old.

　　Begot in, ah, God's ego we go well
Till, ill begun, O sight begone, we die.
Glow, blind worm, seed of that worm-eaten oak
Whose scattered marrow lines my wailing wall,
Yet from my death-beds, fly:
For I with ice-capped bee in outcropped lime
Am etched into hard time
Like diamonds trailing shucks of common coal:—
God's chemical to lesser dust withdraws,
His basilisk dissolves, chimerical
Light lacing light, while through frankincensed air's
Pin-pointless more or less,
Downcast, trumped up, the bored archangel blares.

How is it, ghost, that fin by fur I fare
Your Christ-crossed voyage yet arrive still born?
Packed in my brain your rod and sepulchre
Mark the dim stations of the way I come
Toward my lost other father, my lost home,
Yet wake to find a curling embryo:
But O, perhaps we know—
More than we know. . . . How does the mantis pray?
Does he not fix his dark Silurian eye,
Stark ebony, on the revolving day,
His mechanism pulleyed and well-strung,
And with precise antennae cautiously
Tuned all a-twitch to his predaceous wing,
Drink the charged space with vast humility?

Ice is my sometime high time home, where bone
On cross-bone breeds the issue I would save
Though in my time's sick house I squander it.
So minded may I not, spare head of wit,
By foul means brought to these dead ends alive,
From troubled meanings strike the singleton?
God is the verb by whither out of whence
(Heigh-ho hosanna on Nirvana's couch)
Intransitive, yet active past pretense.
This nothing infinitely out of touch,
Spontaneous mote that kindled waters once,

Spies on the guilt-flecked whites of inner eyes
And drops a saint's-bait hook. "Deliverance,"
My ancient cries, and shakes the astonished trees:
"I found this notion in a lily-pond,
And with a rib-like wand
Divined it for mine, umbilicus and crown:
Then on the stagnant pond the pregnant sun
Showed one preponderant lily and I knew;
Wherefor my knucklebones cracked in His praise;
And like to like my face looked in His face."

Old adamantine clay, dearly though I hold
Your myth and office, and your fall reflect,
Your matter's seasoned well but not well-told.
Before God's creature walked
His foetus somersaulting like a clown
Arrived here upside down;
His question was, not Shall I be foreborne?
But How may I forebear what I am born?
Through the wet nurseries of the fig leaf one
Sweet wind distributed his song and story;
No sooner sung than sorry;
In speaking bush and philosophic stone,
He cut a finite figure twice his size;
The grave stone spoke, a little whittled wood
Grew out of hand and into Paradise;

He thought there were two sides to every grave
Mark of his design, and overweighed with love,
Put out his vessels of propitious blood.

  Time-honored, O false fathered, dreaming you,
I fell through swells, ripped tide and undertow,
Ebb following on flow, the blind crab's house
Of furbelow that holds him far below:
"See! Sea-changed one," I said, "how the light goes!"
Alas, a sea-horse blue
As silence floating by was all his word;
So we become each other after all
(In time or late, as time alone will tell);
All ways my only now, I said or heard:
"Because I fell what me befalls, I will,
And will withal, in fly-blown amber guard
My yard of bones from senseless pyramids!
My word it was crowned the concentric Word
Combustible ditch-water simmered toward,
My fate it was unwound love's foetal cord.
Whirled word! and syllabus of all that hides
Manslaughter, the dog and go and do God
Might from his mill's almighty grindstone free.
Yet I am one. One moves me. None may die;
For all I know, horizons crossing me
My course at three crossroads pike vertical;

O when that cross is twirled, whereon I lie,
My hair and hide bound on the brain-racked wheel
Illusion spins, may fly wherefor and why;
As painted figures on a rolling ball
Show in their turns as one, I shall be whole;
—Yet still this bloodshot globe's an eyeball by
Mind's dead-eye dark blacked out, unless I say."

Goodbye, god-father; sons go on their own
In the long run; farewell, old potentate,
Old lion-heart; though I know woebegone
And prophetless travail avail me nought.
Cast-off of dust, I bolt your five-barred gate
Once more, and clapped anew, through avenues
Of sand-stormed hours spilled time-counterwise,
Fall backwards back to the embalming lake
Where cold, infertile, the moon's eye keeps one
Twin cradle with the whole soft seed of man.
O bridegroom floating in the white bride's wake,
O mirror-peeling, moon-appalling face,
Your fire falls, locked antlers in the bough,
As over cowls of snow,
Arising, haloed with hot sapphire and ice,
First-born offspring of metamorphosis,
I ride my beast-king Christ through Paradise;
Yet will taboos their cutthroat totems raise,

And soon in bloodsoaked sorrow Sophocles
Will publish my dead issue and its name.
O fatal apple of your father's eye,
At this core of the matter lies your dream.
Ah well, ill-webbed or well this net plots my
Hell-bent heyday,—coiled from the eggshell skull,
Foundering truth of that profound doom's day
Dumbfounding all, boomeranged bone again,
Whistling fissions howl through God's cracked bowl;
Who loves his life leaves well enough alone,
Holding his tongue at Pentecost of death,
While somewhere shuttling slowly something weaves
For saw-toothed worms his rag bag mummy cloth,
—Sleep soundly, doom's man, sleep, and be dream's
       child:
—For, when all's twice told, all told we lie cold.

  Stone rolling, cocksure morning, show my son,
And eastering, and westering, at full sail,
Touch these cold stones with specular design;
Toward my lean amplitude be bountiful,
With cockerel quill entablature such rule
As will prevail, and fill with blowing grain
The horn that bids the rakish wedding guest;
When worse comes to the worst, at your behest
Let wine-and-water's sons and daughters mix;

Bless, with good-natured artifice and wit,
Hands that would tend minds our mismarriage breaks,
And over guilt-edged beds long overwrought
Hang emblems from your seamless canopy.
Pull the reluctant water-coddled boy
Up by his roots, and shape his fungus foot
This way, and that way, so long as he may
Find his way forward by his afterthought.
Shine, androgyne, old soloist of dawn;
Your forelocked heirs arise, and on death's bane
Their life-spans overarch, where in the world
Inhuman nature bears one human child.

Host to the worm who'll entertain my clay,
I face my love's child on the face of earth;
His eye's all sea as I remember sea
Where swordfish minnows shred God's images;
His song, swan song, pealed from the stripling tree
Fills my last breath whereon his mouth must close;
As the bough burns, the seed explodes in air:
Wherever I walk now, I wake not here.

Note. To his analysis of "The Worm in the Whirling Cross," published in *A Critical Supplement to Poetry*, November, 1947, John Frederick Nims has brought perspectives which may be of use to other readers. His interpretation of the poem correctly establishes several of my intentions and, sometimes with undue generosity, credits my references. I am indebted to him for permission to reprint here his analysis of the first stanza: "The *logos* is the Logos or 'Word' of the Gospel according to St. John: 'In the beginning was the Word . . .' It equals, in Webster's untechnical summary, 'the actively expressed, creative, and revelatory thought and will of God'—identified, as St. John uses it, with Christ, seen as God made flesh (this poem is partly about a flesh-spirit relationship). But though the logos is the Son, it is also *fathering* in the sense that Christ is the father of men; it is *withering* (punningly applied to *son* instead of to 'sun') not only in that it is destructive of every antagonistic principle but in that adherence to the Logos demands suppression of the excesses of selfhood.

"The first two lines mean that the poet will no longer confess, as graceless and sinful, the activities of his flesh or 'sense.' 'Confess my sins' is the usual phrase; the poet, punningly and concisely, writes *confess my sense*. This is a kind of portmanteau syntax analogous to Lewis Carroll's portmanteau words: 'slithy' = 'lithe' + 'slimy.' In this poem the frequent use of puns may have functional value beyond the richness and ambivalence of meaning they achieve: just as the poem is concerned . . . with identity, so the poet uses puns, semantic devices of identity and nonidentity, to emphasize this aspect of his complex investigation. A somewhat similar purpose is served by the 'further' 'father' 'wither' sounds of the first line: the half-rhymes are not only ornamental but help to convey a sense of the incantation, complexity, and riddle appropriate to the theme.

"*Vouch* means 'to attest, as a statement or its truth or accuracy; bear witness to; also, to answer or stand sponsor for.' The *matter of decaying green* is the *sense* of the preceding line: it means flesh in distinction to spirit: it is called *green* because (1) green is the color of decay, and all flesh is ephemeral, on the verge of decay; (2) green is a vegetation color, and the life of mere flesh, without spirit, is akin to the life of vegetation; (3) green has other relevant connotations: ignorance, envy, illness, and so on. *Matter* is a pun; it means not only 'affair' but 'purulent substance.' *The roof-tree of my dwelling place* is apparently the highest part of the human structure, the skull. The *shark's tooth grin*, a fresh but appropriate symbol for the leer of a fleshless skull, is fastened, or *hinged*, to the *roof-tree* by the *decaying green* of the flesh. Flesh, then, is an ambiguous principle; it covers, in both a benignant and a sinister sense, the grinning skull; decadent itself, it makes whole and secure the dwelling place of the human spirit. In summary, the first five lines of the poem express an acceptance of the life of flesh and sense as indispensable in spite of their imminent corruption.

"The apple (line 6) is the fruit, traditionally an apple, the eating of which led to Adam and Eve's expulsion from the garden of innocence. *Apple-wise* suggests three meanings: (1) like an apple, i.e., possessing only unconscious vegetable life; (2) wise (partially in an ironic sense, as in 'wise guy') in the way of apples, i.e., knowing about the apple of Eden and capable of making an independent decision about it; (3) wise with the sad wisdom that came from eating the forbidden apple on the Tree of Knowledge of Good and Evil. The line means that man learned anguish in Eden, . . . a mythological way of saying in a primal state of innocence or unselfconsciousness (*the first sun*—which may also mean the *son* of line 1). The next two lines are an analysis or further explanation of the change and the consequent mourning: the giraffes perhaps symbolic of the ungainly but interesting barbaric *élan* of pre-conscious life; the Tigris a recollection (of course

39

anachronistic) of a center of man's early activity, but, as *spring* indicates, there is also intended a pun on tiger, which has a powerful symbolic force in itself and is immeasurably reinforced by recollections of two of the great tigers of literature: Blake's beautiful terror in the forests of the night and Eliot's tiger in 'Gerontion': 'In the juvescence of the year/ Came Christ the tiger . . .'

"The ninth line, given vehemence by the exclamatory 'O' which precedes it, identifies more precisely, in tracing more accurately, the source of the anguish. It is not only the double disaster (Fall and Flood) of Genesis; it is, more profoundly, the event of individual genesis, of personal birth. When the human being, at a fell swoop, leaves the prenatal lake he is born to anguish: *genesis* repeats the pattern of 'Genesis.' Here Brinnin seems to infuse his Christian symbolism with the notion of happy pre-existence (cf. Wordsworth's 'Imitations'). At any rate, man's innocence and wholeness (or 'identity') have been lost at an early stage of his history.

"The tenth line wonders how they can be rediscovered in our time. *Ray* no longer means what it meant for Milton; a ray (X-ray, etc.) is a modern method of discovery for healing. It is possible that 'excellent' here affords an ironic comment on the inadequacy of science to deal with the spirit.

"In line eleven, the *you* refers most probably to the *logos* of the beginning. To learn how *leaf mould burns*, that is, how the vestiges or last survivals of vegetative life achieve (1) splendor; (2) a proper and natural termination, one must *cross grain with* be grafted to, coöperate with (in spite of the dissonant hints of the adjective 'cross-grained') the logos or Christ, the highest embodiment of knowledge in a human form. The *dome's dove-tailing brows* again describes the skull with its beautiful articulations: when Christ was killed, it seems to say, his personal vision or *inscape* revealed new human vistas, new possibilities of human existence. As large waves (groundswells) are stirred up by earthquakes or other undersea disasters, so the individual is excited, by the example of the logos, to welcome the violences of the life of the flesh, which the logos had also undergone."

THE

SORROWS

OF

COLD

STONE *

---

* These acrostics were not designed to be read as portraits.

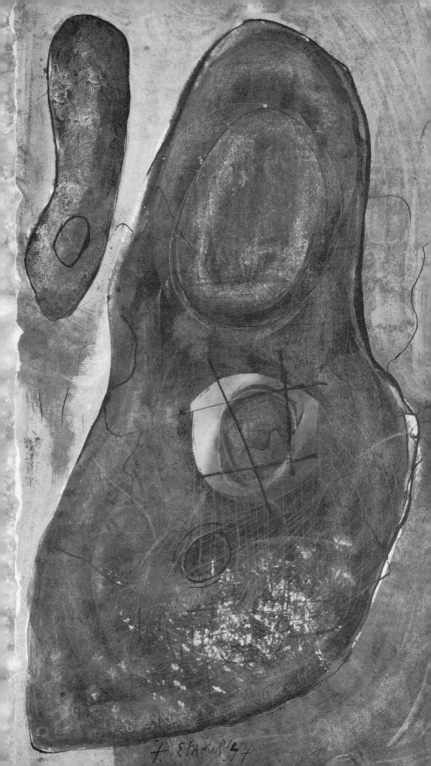

As, Adamant, My Bones Were Ground, My Hand

As, adamant, my bones were ground, my hand
Lay down; as, chained, my hawk-red eye was tamed
From branch to wrist, my brooding feathers found
Roost underground; as, loved, I fell redeemed,
Elated fingers peeled me like a wand,
Divined my name and called my coming doomed.

Green is that garment I would wear again—
Ribbed leaf, loose tendril curling from the ripe
Armpit and groin, with good grass at the lip
Yoked soberly to chaff my witty grain.

But I, of weed the widower thonged by flesh
Unfit, in loin-cloth, sack-cloth, mummy-cloth,
Race my green wish. O ever-burning bush,
Root deep, O as death bates, bate, bait this breath.

Grave Mind I Loved, of All
Who Mind Your Grave

Grave mind I loved, of all who mind your grave
Or lie beside, I know that John Donne's ghost
Recants the dying falls, the skull-capped love
Deaths and quick rime that—how long since!—would try
Our inarticulate mortality,
Needling for dust the flesh we favored most.

Sleep sound, sweet foundling, though I'd sound your sleep;
Make what you will of metaphysic bone,
I will not mind. Until my time is up,
Take heart, my heart, if a ghost may have one,
Have done with John's thin image and have Donne.

The Blue Swan from Wyoming to Peru

The blue swan from Wyoming to Peru
Resumes, one feather lost, his cold patrol;
Upswept at times, at times volplaning low,
Mountain whitecaps bend his single sail,
And yet, for so much loss, his shadow hangs
Nightlong on rock, and daylong lines his wings.

Captivity of self, like the guitar's
Abundant silences, attracts the wind
Put forth for sorrow, the grief that wears
Only the landscape proper to its kind.
This folded bird, for all he bear another,
Endures a blizzard in one falling feather.

Rockpool and Ice-Haired Ledge Paint Images

Rockpool and ice-haired ledge paint images
Upon the Sistine cobalts of the sea;
This is an Eden, gull's egg and genesis,
Here's the flat crab's dead-drunk Gethsemane.

Vortex and spiral whistling into blue
Environs through the undertows of space
Needle the whale-back box and coffin through;
As in the beauty of the rocks' duress
Burdens of time are tattered like a seine,
Love, sloughing its granite thighs and mouths of stone,
Endures a slow unstitching bone by bone.

Chill as a Winter Gull, Mind's Lawless Bell

Chill as a winter gull, mind's lawless bell
Outrides the clattering water-clocks of space;
Now like a shark, now like a ray, it pulls
Sense from its tender mooring in the race,
Tangles the sober eye and ear, sing-song,
And piques the lovers' grove with wind-flushed tongue
Nibbling at ecstasy. Its highs and lows
Charge winter's solstice with the summer's rose,
Enter the equinox and give it snows.

Still in that archness there's a constancy
Makes wantonness a lesson we shall keep;
In the gray cage where lynx and lion mope
Those echoes teach our mortal anarchy,
Hoisting a bone upon the banks of sleep.

Hailing the rib-shaped taxi, fingering keys
On bonewhite stairways leading to a place
Where music is, hands learn the world at loss
And feel the way back through slow galleries;
Rooms open, portraits cough but, ah, they fail;
Daylight meets dark upon the melting wall.

Mild as an awning in a mist, the face
Of mystery dies and dreams its other house,
Something not built about an axle-tree,
Something a child cuts from his memory.

Vermeer, of light the constant Gabriel,
Extends the morning on his scales of gold,
Repairs the flounder-face and dragging bell
Night pulls full-fathomed in its swarming fold;
Outside, the wheels of morning wind and go
Nowhere; the nighthawk winds no longer blow.

Vendor and relic of what vanishes,
Enchanted by slow time that stops in space,
Naked he comes and from the shade abstracts
Annunciation. So richly doomed, he dies
By perfectness; in its paralysis
Lies locked until like radium his eyes
Eat through the dark the dark alone reflects.

Kiss of the tree, the improbable gold apple,
Admonishes, "The heart of man must kill,"
Yet morning shows no violence at all.

My heart, though Eden beats as you beat still,
Unless within transfixed self-sight you die
Head high, the fiction of that preposterous fall
Serves not at all, and cold roots eat the tree.

By Glory, Said the Greek, and Omens Fell

By Glory, said the Greek, and omens fell
In bird-bone alphabets on the whirlpool—
Lightly the zeta floated, lightly the psi,
Lightly the hollow amens of prophecy.

Riddled and reft, poor raddled skeletons
Enter the flotsam delta time discards;
At long length, on the esplanade of bones,
Designs of Greeks cross-stitch the signs of birds.

Could we but lift a white hand on this day
Or flag the hawk from love's metropolis,
No dawning would be shelled, no midnight lie
Stalemated on the clocks of holiday;
This wisdom that we worry so would smile
At singlest hollyhock and looting bird,
Noting how all's in nettings yet unbound,
Caught in earth's charity as in a wheel
Entangled fortune swings, and say no word.

Evil is that largesse of innocence
Life into life its moats and castles twines;
Love squanders love, it cuts a royal wound.
In spite of all we know, in stealth we're found
Starting a suture for what will not mend.

Knife is the name. To write in less than blood
Is harlotry of intellect unless
Mind make of madness music in the wood,
Of music madness in its own excuse;
Nothing can sing that is not fed with blood.

Find orchids; from their human screams uproot
Relics of wolf's-jaw, wings of unfeathered bone;
In rockface carve the grottoes of man's fate
And cross its Christ-thorn knuckles on the plain.
Ruin alone keeps God's ramshackle gate.

Pretense Employs Us, Innocence Must Lie

Pretense employs us, innocence must lie
Enmeshed with swan unblinking, fox of flame;
Nothingness enfolds us, in its smothering eye
Entranced, like nuns, we marry into time
Lest time neglect us, or the brows of space
Obliterate our mast-and-spar faced calm.
Primates of fern, granite our parish is;
Ensigns of Capricorn, the cold's our home.

Pretense puts music on our minor afternoons
Elusive as a carousel of sounds
Around the flights of foxes chasing swans
Rising and falling. The lightnings of mischance
Light all we live with; we must have pretense.

Mine Is a Voyage on a Cloudless Eye

Mine is a voyage on a cloudless eye
Adapted to that surface as a skate
Round which the flakes from bowsprit never fly;
Gardens so jailed with frost and salt they fight
All summer toward the waterfalls are mine,
Rivers whose smooth meandering thumbs can press
Enormous homesteads from a wilderness;
The comet's swan-like after-tow is mine.

Time comes and goes and what was never snow
Hangs like a thousand seagulls in a hall
Of glass. O in that tinder stillness blue
Madonnas burn like lamps profane as pitch,
Philosophy's great odalisques who dwell
Sun-centered in their own phosphor. To touch
Or dream them is to fuse that greening kiss
No mouth returns, no tongue relinquishes.

Bless Martyrs of This Time
Whose Madness Is

Bless martyrs of this time whose madness is
Essential coat-of-arms and crown to this
Vast mummery, bless even the child whose eye
Engages Satans of delight and grows
Resourceful in their profane circuses;
Love what you can and leave the rest awry;
Your pity wants a false menagerie.

Beware the thoughtful citizen of clay
And unicorns in their heraldic pride,
For on the pennants of the time's decay
Fly fire and ice, the world's first groom and bride.

Jacks and Jills Who Find the Day's Eyes Gone

Jacks and Jills who find the day's eyes gone,
Old buckets split with grassblades, shattered crowns
Hurled everywhichway in a masque of death,
Neglect, as every man and woman, omens

That say the rack of ecstasy's a wraith;
Hand in hand, contracted to and fro,
Over the routes of carrion they go
Misleading all their need. Love's minute is
Primrose promise to their flying chase,
So simple to the mouths that touch it there
Only the tongues of nightshade seem much softer.
Now, when they have it, they twice tumble after.

By rational shallows which the soughing seawall
Answers with a groan, cast in his sorrows,
Stands the sad savage. O useless arrows
Inked with herb and sulphur, I know how all
Love's sharpest flintings are made neutral.

Read it in war and skull-faced cockleshells:
Anchorage anywhere's all hazardous
Unless, from zany undermottled meadows,
Creatures who keep the sea's preposterous schools
Hold sails in chains before the world's windswells.

Burning, the Corse Spoke Through
Its Mouth of Flame

Burning, the corse spoke through its mouth of flame.
It said, I am the torch love puts to time;
Love feeds on air, it said, flame forks its root,
Lose love, it said, and all that is is not.

Rain ashes now, come frost-faced nothingness,
Undo my glazed heart from these hissing bones;
Charge me at zero, make me less and less
Hospitable to anacrostic stones.
Tell me, O silences of salt, say what
I said upon that flaming chariot.

Jerked from its shell limp and impossible—
O most humiliating mimicry—
Her sex or his both indiscernible,
Naked, the self-loved snail prepares to die.

Repelled by such constructions of the sea
Our flesh, mnemonic, crawls away;
Buried, the wild heart leaps its curved rib-cage;
Immured, the fish-ghost in the thin blood swims
Nibbling a current thought cannot assuage;
Swift through the tree of nerves, the red light streams
On memories dissolved in memory:
Naked, self-loved, we witness how we die.

Think of That Place Among All Buried Places

Think of that place among all buried places,
Hideout of dog and angel: there children stand
Eternal, mindless, in the bandaged dress
Old scarecrows hurl, all sleeves, against the wind;
Dead-white, with sad top-heavy heads entwined,
Of love the monuments, love-locked they fall
Root, rib and swaddling cerement one grave,
One tidal wave the fishing moon's long pull
Shores like a cockleshell but cannot save.

Sun of their sleep, the good year's native light
Tunes the young engines of earth's changelessness,
And through the world's veined head, all moss and eyes,
Mortality unwinds—night after night
On mandrake roots to dream, half man, half tree,
Saying to scarecrow children, Wait for me.

Mystery, like a glass bird in a box,
Assails the space that yet encloses it;
Remote, at ease come cage or paradox,
Yonder the pure shapes of mere wonder float.

Wonder, strange pond where drift the dim, sad swans,
And the ancient turtle paddles in the lily bed,
Lays ghost by Holy Ghost; while through that once
Known water's hyssop of puerperal blood,
Evil the mystery, feathering a thought,
Rattles like God its little bonewhite foot.

Architect, Logician, How Well the Snail

Architect, logician, how well the snail
Narrates its tenuous predicament!
Knit with fragility, its echoing cowl
Enlarges hope as love indentures want,
Yet holds its heart like water in a bowl.

Like those who temper opal for a house
A wise man keeps the cosmos in his skull
Rimmed with a box of sound where every day
Repeats his wishing yet confirms him whole.
As flesh grows merry in its neutral shell,
Beware the pleasures of small bones that fit
Elbow to brow when the design's not whole;
Each hauls his house; the trick's to live in it.

THE

ABHORRED

AFFECTIONS

The Verb

Unuttered as it was was but to love,
To love not the brief constancy, to love
Not the presentiment and aftermath of
Love but, rage of it, possession.

To love the ample circle circling still
And so to love that which, as violable
As innocence, makes mystery visible,
The knowledge of unknowing.

As all at once assembling from nowhere
Birds of a white anonymous featherage are
Snow over water, my ambitions were
Wheeling toward descent, one wing.

In that snow-blinding air, so purely come
To love what sense-beyond-idea, like time
Leased from its calendar, had warned me from,
Sleeping I watched your sleep.

O in that turning saying be and do,
To love was but self-knowledge, knowing you
Dreamed on a glass-blown sill as though
The walls of my sleep mirrored you.

My real, unravelled, ravelled out of space,
To love you is to wake and, as it is,
By love undreamed alive, I touch your face
Knowing the meaning, loving, being loved.

A Love Song for Ash Wednesday

Darling, our dust,
Which death with other dust will bed,
On Wednesday last,
When, *mea culpa*, mankind fed
On common matter, common thread,
Went privately instead.

Your shadowed smile
At length in shadow-play crossed mine,
To hold me while
Mouths full of ashes sang Amen
And bone with bone in doom's dust-bin
Clapped heartbreak in.

Cold serpents pealed,
Like whistling flutes birds lighted off,
Bare trees grown old
In the dead springtime took new leaf.
For the rest of his long-winded life
About us, death was safe.

His time's to waste
Who will, ere long, make waste of us.
Why, then, this haste
To lay unsettled dust? What used
Do we rehearse, what truth impress
But, naked, nakedness?

70

This much is ours
That soon dispersed and much the same
Will crowd, of course,
His subconventions of dark loam;
But upright, quick, far from our home,
Sack-cloth wears tiresome.

Wind shall not sift
These well-banked ashes quite so soon.
While time is left
To sleep supine we'll lay us down
Beside, still prone to entertain,
All ways, what lies between.

Turning, returning on world winds that know
The fondled matter of a time ago,
My bondsman angel with spread-eagle eye
Reminds my wounds, unwinds my reveille;
Within a cleft of sleep
Where the abhorred affections, arm in arm,
Lion and tamer come,
The ways I went, the days I could not keep
Stand still: wrapt in perfect ice I lie
Creating love out of a masque of clay
And see my arms, like vines, embrace a city.

O lion locked in yesterday, O lost
And by the years' five-shuttered cages last
Of all my lives, be fed on memory
Though, starved, you waken and go free;
Of your own flesh and blood,
The hand that froze mid-air, the heart that sank,
Make present meat and drink
That by your providence the sweet ghost laid
In love's misfitting batter at the door
Closed fast upon the only traveler
Hand would warm at, heart be lifted for.

Indentured angel, show me where I go
Though in long dwelling I imprison you;

In ponds of sleep, in pools of sense, over
Whatever solvent water you will hover,
Trouble the seines whose turning
Pictures on the water's winding wheel
Show now and always how all
Traveling is a leaving no returning
Though hands like spindrift fall awash before
Wheel, gear, piston rod and wild propeller
Rifle the air to make farewell forever.

For My Pupils in the War Years

To come to a congress of books when thoughtless death
Spoils the small chances of your happiness
Is an old, perhaps academic, idea of truth;
And yet, in the small matter of a page,
Young as you are, and centered otherwise,
The instructions of the dead attest your privilege.

Turning their difficult honors in your hands
As jewelers turn stones, your eyes reprove
Those radical loves and that extravagance
Of spirit under the brightness of dubious gods;
For yours is the climate of a budding grove
In whose dissolving summer learned impasse fades.

Surely the world's not glorious for facts
In a conqueror's litany of taken places
On the map of total loss. Though times like these elect
Their minor offices to classic fame,
In the smoking fields of second choices
The arch and ruined porch shall be your home.

Since greatness is unfinished and somewhat foolish
In its dead pretensions, you are not involved;
Romantic agonies become your lavish
Idea of a child playing bride on rainy days,
Or the valentine mystery that was never solved
Until you were older, and had moved to another house.

When rebels ride to action, you remain.
Yet through the anger of your innocence,
Accomplished and free, they will ride back again.
Their guilt is brave, and when you can believe it,
With a cold grace you will take their adult hands;
For there is nothing to learn about death but how to
    achieve it.

Love in Particular

When the orchard that clings to the terrace is boxed
      for the winter
And birds take the sun deck and the first hieroglyph of snow
Sprawls on the darkening side street under crawling cars,
    There is much to be reconsidered
    About the nature of this place;
    Because of all doomed capitals
    Certainly none was less
    Love's climate or to its light more false.

In the encroaching blue of its twilight, the exciting
Approach of still another enormous evening, how many
Desolate figures watch the first lights of Radio City
    Burn for a little while—
    As those who in great harbors
    Framed in a thousand portholes
    Attend the huge maneuverings of liners
    And the infinitesimal farewells?

Each to his own fake fireplace, each to his hobby
Of glass elephants that trumpet in duplicate herds
Across twenty square inches of table-top mirror,
    While the modest leaf of love
    Fumes like a steaming orchid
    In the center of the room,
    Costly, rootless, and naked,
    And disappears like flame.

Ah, the swift matings and undernourished affections,
The pledge of troth as tidy as a business deal
Of unexpected advancement with a comfortable eq-
        uity;
    In their profitless commerce at midnight,
    Pulverous shadows strive
    To gain their random image,
    While bartenders give them nerve
    And the bankers give homage.

To admit that this is not an accident but an achievement
Is but to marry St. Patrick's to the Onyx Club
With dancing afterward and mingling of the guests,
    For in the sacrifice of appetite,
    The angel of love hangs in the sky
    Like a corpse of warning;
    Many murders are in his eye
    Every blessed morning.

The lights and lives that stratify these avenues
Shine at the frayed nerve ends of a prodigious hunger
Not to be answered by a million appetites
    For love without identity
    Or burned to exhaustion in a night
    Of gaiety and anger,
    For the anarchies of appetite
    Are not the feasts of hunger.

Leave it, then, to an impromptu drift of snow,
Some falling, final graciousness of snow
That brings its trophies and mistakes to burial;
    If to begin again
    Means other faces, other ambitions,
    Love is as long as time
    And as full of notions.
    Let the day perish, let the day come.

Rowing in Lincoln Park

You are, in 1925, my father;
Straw-hatted, prim, I am your only son;
Through zebra-light fanwise on the lagoon
Our rented boat slides on the lucent calm.

And we are wistful, having come to this
First tableau of ourselves: your eyes that look
Astonished on my nine bravado years,
My conscious heart that hears the oar-locks click

And swells with facts particular to you—
How France is pink, how noon is shadowless,
How bad unruly angels tumbled from
That ivory eminence, and how they burned.

And you are vaguely undermined and plan
Surprise of pennies, some directed gesture,
Being proud and inarticulate, your mind
Dramatic and unpoised, surprised with love.

In silences hermetical as this
The lean ancestral hand returns, the voice
Of unfulfillment with its blade-like touch
Warning our scattered breath to be resolved.

And sons and fathers in their mutual eyes
Exchange (a moment huge and volatile)

The glance of paralytics, or the news
Of master-builders on the trespassed earth.

Now I am twenty-one and you are dead,
And late in Lincoln Park the rowers cross
Unfavored in their odysseys, the lake
Not dazzling nor wide, but dark and commonplace.

A Letter

A day was nothing until this; words went
Like horns through traffic, like the instant birds;
A day was dormant, yet-to-be-danced among
The sudden neon furniture and books.

It was that intricate familiar thing
When, coughing like the French ambassador,
The postman said his phrase about the rain
And went undeviating through the door.

O, if I wanted legacies, a poem,
An invitation to the dance, or hoped
For declarations of a stranger's love,
My fingers burst like matches on your name.

If it is later now, if the rain has stopped,
If no one dressed in seaweed lurches in
Like some surprised Ophelia with green hands,
I covet reason but for truth like this:

There is communication on the earth
As quiet as the opening of a wing;
There is a wine of choice, and we who drink
Touch all our future to that emphasis.

Who winds the clumsy flower-clock now, I wonder,
And opens the minaret in Waterworks Park
For bird's-eye views of captive fern and reindeer?
"Heavy heavy heavy hangs over thy head,"
The flower-clock said,
"What shall ye do to redeem it?"

Do conch shells hum in shingled bungalows
Where stop-streets subdivide eternity?
Has the crutch bloomed in St. Bartholomew's?
Crazy as preachers, running all night long,
Do empty street cars still go off their trolleys
Trailing brimstone, tolling cling and clang?
"Heavy heavy heavy hangs over thy head,"
The trolley-car said,
"What shall ye do to redeem it?"

And there were sea-gulls that far from the sea!
Once, I recall, on the soft river air,
Like a hovering Holy Ghost, one talked to me.
It was a night in spring, when ice-floes rolled
Like foggy castles in the melting rain.
"Heavy heavy heavy hangs over thy head,"
The ice-floes said,
"What shall ye do to redeem it?"

I called it my home-town, I guess, although
Constantinople seems more plausible.
I wonder if the night-shift lights still glow
Like sea-fires in a shipwrecked neighborhood.
I wonder if some still-eyed ten-year-old
Goes sidewise on the sea-floor as I did.
"Heavy heavy heavy hangs over thy head,"
The night lights said,
"What shall ye do to redeem it?"

Must time so rage behind that I still go
Face-down forever toward some small event?
And does my echo know what once I knew?
"Heavy heavy heavy hangs over thy head,"
The echo, echoing, said,
"What shall ye do to redeem it?"

Little Elegy for Gertrude Stein

Pass gently, pigeons on the grass,
For where she lies alone, alas,
Is all the wonder ever was.

Deeply she sleeps where everywhere
Grave children make pink marks on air
Or draw one black line . . . here to there.

Because effects were upside down,
Ends by knotty meanings thrown,
Words in her hands grew smooth as stone.

May every bell that says farewell,
Tolling her past all telling tell
What she, all told, knew very well.

If now, somehow, they try to say—
This way, that way, everywhichway—
Goodbye . . . the word is worlds away.

Come softly, all; she lies with those
Whose deepening innocence, God knows,
Is as the rose that is a rose.

Speech of the Wedding Guest

FOR TOM AND KAY

O random dove that binds its kissing kin,
   Entwinéd bird, most linked with written gold,
By this discretion among choices be
   That severing wind that doth unmarry me.

For singleness as witness to the fact
   Knows the full price, yet wary of the cost,
Makes benedictions with the best of heart
   Blessing the sea by which it stands apart.

So, soft aloft and lighting, dithering bird,
   This ritual of love and goods demands
Meticulous attendance to make mute
   The hither and yawning of the mourning flute.

By your good office, two once met as two
   Are joined and doubled to become unique;
Yet would you be incautious to outstay
   The fluttering homiletics of the day.

As night falls to renew the whispering green
   Of the first fell garden where your feathers shone,
Be off, pert package, to your own dove-cote
   And give free ribbon to their chariot.

Be watchful of my dark; I will watch yours.
    For by this mating we are met alone,
Cohabitors of nought or, if we please,
    Of furnished rooms in the antipodes.

When bursting from a bell you wheel on streets
    Mosaic with confetti, blinds still drawn,
Brood not that, heedless of your hermitage,
    A rumpled sheet has ratified a pledge.

Yours was the moment frozen in the dance.
    Another music carries you away.
O in that measure bless what you can bless
    And light, for my part, upon singleness.

LOCAL

INSTANCES

not an attitude
but a climate—
   native riviera
   where light, pale but successful, spots
      a lank destroyer stopped in a gorgeous calm,
      or a shark-like sloop.

Nothing predicted
her, unless the
   sea did, tossing, like a
   diamond in Kansas, a mil-
      limeter's labyrinth of coral on the
      tides of Rockaway;

unless another
age did, when, in
   a sky-blue vestal gown
   and ice-blue jockey cap (the stripes
      were meaningless, the sporting kings were dead) she
      rode a merry race

near Paris in the
Degas steeplechase,
   figuratively, of
   course. Vision cracked with a pin, its
      voyages at a standstill, its purposes
      exposed yet honored—

polarities that
span the world, while
   Yankee-jawed camels, the
   chariest most north-of-Boston
      types, scheme through the needle's eye to find, if not
      their proper heavens,

facsimiles there-
of. It is not
   that another couldn't
   match her method of embalming
      mirrors but that, like so much which passes for
      life in Brooklyn, she

happened there first. To
an age of art-
   ifice she brings laurels
   of artifact. How special, then,
      are these few poems of a rectitude so
      insular they will

be saved as saints are
saved whose palms bleed
   annually, because
   like the glass flowers at Harvard
      (lessons in perfect lifelessness) they are what
      they're talking about.

To the Priest in the Window Seat

Father, we have left the ground
You smudged my forehead with one darker Wednesday,
    And now the Te Deum laudamus sound
Of four cowled Pratt and Whitney engines sends my
    Thoughts toward years when, in your charge,
I felt the tendrils of my soul grown large
    Beyond the husbandry I could command,
And heard you, muffled in a cloth,
Forgive my sins with a half-lifted hand,
And teach me how elastic was our faith.

Never did I think we'd meet
With both feet in the air nor, parted, share—
    Two thirds of trinity—a triple seat,
Nor guess that, in this Appalachian air,
    The same assumption would not hold
For both of us. And yet, as if foretold
    In that sly preference of opposites
For what will undermine them, we exchange
A journey's pleasantries of smiles and lights
And, parallel, refuse to find them strange.

If I, like that black angel, Joyce,
Have for the millionth time gone forth to meet
    Reality, to forge in my soul not grace
But this world's unborn conscience, is not fate

The heresy on which we part?
What I have mind for, you can have no heart.
    Still, by this dedicated waywardness,
I feel strangely at one with you,
A prodigal whose silence is, like yours,
Uplifted by the grandeur of the view.

    Two souls in mortal flight, we take
Sustaining morsels from a pillowed tray
    And, on heaven's business and the world's, sit back
To think on whence we came and where we go.
    Midwestern sunlight blinds us now,
And while we cannot see our wings, we know
    By a long-travelled faith they are still there.
I shall miss you, father, and may want your pity,
When you go on toward higher ground somewhere,
And I get off, as planned, in Kansas City.

Nuns at Eve

On St. Martin's evening green
Imaginary diamond, between
The vestry buttress and the convent wall,
Solemn as sea-birds in a sanctuary,
Under the statue of the Virgin they play baseball.
They are all named Mary,
Sister Mary, Mary Anthony or Mary Rose,
And when the softball flies
In the shadow of the cross
The little chaplet of the Virgin's hands
Contains their soft excitements like a house.

A flying habit traces
The unprecedented rounding of the bases
By Sister Mary Agatha, who thanks God
For the easy triple and turns her eyes toward home;
As *Mary, Mother, Help Me* echoes in her head,
Mild cries from the proud team
Encourage her, and the obliging sun,
Dazzling the pitcher's box
With a last celestial light upon
The gold-spiked halo of the Virgin in her niche,
Leads Sister Mary John to a wild pitch.

Prayer wins the game.
As Sister Mary Agatha comes sailing home

Through infield dusk, like birds fan-wise
In the vague cloisters of slow-rising mist,
Winners and losers gather in to praise
The fleetness of a bride of Christ.
Flushed and humble, Agatha collects the bats
And balls, while at her belt
Catcher's and pitcher's mitts
—Brute fingers, toes and gross lopsided heads—
Fumble the ropes of her long swinging beads.

American Plan

The antique Indian should be Henry James
    Notebook in hand, a well-disguised impostor;
The porch should (spiritually) face the Thames
    And not the Vineyard or East Gloucester.

The juke-box in the Palm Court should play Herbert
    For ladies quite exhausted from croquet;
The chocolate popsicle should be lime sherbet
    Served in a glass on a hand-painted tray.

The man in the Hawaiian wrap-around
    Should wear white flannels and a State St. boater;
His wife on water-skis across the Sound
    Should make her bread-and-butter calls by motor.

His daughter in the slacks should loll and dally
    Under a parasol from *Maison Worth;*
The things her mad-cap girl-chums say should really
    Put her in stitches, into gales of mirth.

The Cris Craft should be an Old Town Canoe;
    The yellow Jeepster in the *porte cochere*
Should be a Willys-Overland tonneau,
    Equipped with robes, ferns, curtains and a spare.

When rats desert a bather's hair-do, all
    Well-meaning sympathy should quite unnerve her;

To thwart the masher and the ne'er-do-well,
    The bathing dress should be a life-preserver.

Photographers with tripod, hood and birdie,
    Should take group-portraits on the tennis lawn;
The families should look joyless, drawn, but sturdy:
    Men standing, women seated, children prone.

From cupola and minaret should fly
    The flags of summertime, good, old and windswept.
("Gay Whirl at Ocean House" reported by
    The New York Herald and *The Boston Transcript*.)

For jolly times that should be had by all,
    For moonlight sings, for roundelay and ballad,
The picnic launch should leave the boathouse full
    Of citronella and potato salad.

The kodachrome should be a free-hand drawing
    (The bathing beach seen from the bathhouse door)
Showing the sunset on the long withdrawing
    Tide and, dimly, figures on the shore.

Views of the Favorite Colleges

Approaching by the gate, (Class of '79,
All dead) the unimpressed new scholars find
Halls of archaic brick and, if it is April,
Three dazzling magnolias behind bars, like lions.

Unsettling winds among the pillars of wisdom
Assure them of harmonious extremes,
However academic. The bells, in key,
Covered with singing birds, ring on the hour.

Towering, but without aspiration, the campanile
Is known to sway an inch in a high wind;
But that, like the statue's changeable complexion,
Is natural. To find the unnatural,

Gradually absorb the industry
Of ten o'clock: the embryo pig slit through
With the proper instruments by embryos;
And Sophocles cut, for speed, with a blue pencil.

Prehensile sophomores in the tree of learning
Stare at the exiled blossoming trees, vaguely puzzled;
The lecturer, especially if bearded,
Enhances those druidical undertones.

What is the terminus of books? sing the birds.
Tell us about Sophocles! cry the trees.
And a crazy child on roller-skates skates through
The campus like a one-man thunderstorm.

A River

A winkless river of the cloistered sort
Falls in its dark habit massively
Through fields where single cattle troll their bells
With long shows of indifference, and through
The *fêtes champêtres* of trees so grimly bent
They might be gallows-girls betrayed by time
That swung them once on picnics by Watteau.

Electric in its falling, passing fair
Through towns touched up with gilt and whitewash,
It chooses cast-offs, songs and feathers
And the stuff of life that must keep secrets
Everlastingly: the red and rat-like curios
Of passion, knives and silks and embryos
All sailing somewhere for a little while.

The midnight drunkard pausing on the bridge,
Dumbstruck when stories catch his half-closed eye,
Has waterfalls for memories; he must
Command five tottering steeples to be still,
For what he sees pass under him is not
Mere moonlit oil and pods of floating seed,
But, on his soul, a most astonishing swan.

The river, I mean, for all is riverine
Goes slowly inward, as one would say of time,

So it goes, and thus proceed to gather in
The dishes of a banquet, or the bones
Of someone lost in battle yesterday,
Glad in the wisdom of his pity to serve
Though the river's knowledge, whelming, overwhelms.

"The terrible girls have outlived all that silver,"
Said the matron from St. Louis, Mo.,
And the taxi down from Reno every night
Waits by the prefab cottage door
Under the one red light.

"How strange that in this mountain rock the graves
Are marked with wood," said the clerk from Cleveland, O.,
And the worms get through another wind-smooth cross,
And the playbill face of Joseph Jefferson
Peels from the Opera House.

"Buy me a drink where Mark Twain wrote that book,"
Said the blonde from Pasadena, Cal.,
And where the streets fall off into clear sky
The Indian in the G.I. shoes
Watches the Fords go by.

"Look, genuine nuggets from the Comstock Lode,"
Said the dentist from Port Huron, Mich.,
And minerals glitter in his thinning blood
Where death made a killing in the hills
And settled down for good.

"Ten silver dollars for the slot machine,"
Said the bride from Providence, R.I.,
And where the hurricanes of avarice
Once passed, the juke-box in the Last Chance Bar
Opens its silver voice.

At the Airport

Here, at the airport, waiting,
Watching the schedule by
The opulent calm of a match,
I think: the cold, unpeopled stars
This hutch of night that wears
A floodlight for an eye,
Have turned against my hope.

When silence broadens: swinging,
Whipped by the wind, the little
Zeppelins report a change;
And from the glassy tower goes
Immediately its subtle news:
Over the moonlike lakes
Whose wings? Whose ancient name?

On margins of the field, cattle
Make their slow and noiseless rounds,
Imprinting daisies or
A singular cleft hoof in mud;
Degenerate, soft-eyed, they plod
Without expectancy;
Sometimes, even, they sleep.

A signal's up! The humming
Imminence of wings

Berates the thoughtful ear;
I underline my schedule with
A fingernail; across the path
Of light, and lazily,
The great eyes land with pride.

All those I've loved in any
History have come;
Their presence, like a wreath
Of pain, sits coldly on my skull;
Puzzled, resigned to good or ill,
Yet fearing recognition,
I watch them evilly.

Do I dare to greet them, calling
"This is the place, this is
The one who telegraphed?"
Emerging single file, they seem
Like statues scissored from a dream,
Except that in their eyes
The past has turned to stone.

I turn into the City;
Let them wonder who it was
That brought them here, who called
Across the distances as if

Their presence meant his very life;
The City is more kind
With stranger citizens.

Now when I hear my pillow
Hum with those approaching wings,
I remember how they came
Out of the heavenly dark that night;
Only a ghost would choose to wait,
Among the quiet cattle,
Their coming down again.

FOR AUSTIN WARREN

To say, Change Cometh, set the old scene straight,
Mark off long summer in a frame of kites
Pegging the four blue corners of the wind;
So turns my purpose backward, chill with leaves.

Like voyagers who, slow to lose the weave
Of seas beneath them, waver on the shore,
So am I beached upon this running strand
While underwater all Manhattan tolls.

Now shall I range the sands hysterical,
And speak with parables to the swift sun?
My hands are curious, when driftwood comes,
Testing a branch, or tracing lettering.

If, in the manner of the books, some sail
Comes riding over all that scattered loss,
May I rejoice for piracy and thieves,
Beat on a drum, scrimmage for preference?

Go down, my summertime, with every kite
That like a roving anchor drags my heart;
Come, summer like a masterpiece, come sky,
Demand to be remembered, framed and false.

Glorious Victory of the Sloop Maria

Her breastbone bent toward victory, breeze-blue
Maria skirts the offshore barber poles
   And, like a page of music blown,
Slides home all angles with her face-down crew.

First on the line and first across the water,
Maria starts the whole flotilla tooting,
   Circles the candy lighthouse twice,
Then slows at ease in zephyrs of applause.

So glorious it was, all afternoon.
Yet what, in telling, dips as bowsprits do
   Or plunges those white, straining manes
Below, above that spindrift furbelow?

Who feels the wing of summer, summer gone?
What seascape splashes on a clubhouse wall
   When the wind blows or does not blow?
Where is the moment in the framed memento?

No, no. Maria lies in dead seas now,
A flying memory of a victory past,
   Her glorious mainsail stricken short
Between the gun and the far-off retort.

A Bone-White Village in the Savages

I see it upside down:
Pickets and steeples dripping morning light
Through little brush-soft acres of ripe wheat;
I see the housewife cyclist like a fly
Crawling through cabbage-roses toward the white
Green-grocer's marzipan displays
Of unclasped lettuces, grapes bubbling down,
Where paisley-faced Miss Shakespeare, paisley-
    shawled,
Winds toward the post with letters for the dead
And mackerel clouds, close-scalloped like the sea,
Repeat, repeat on rock the sun Cézannes
With just that waver of the brush that means
A mill-pond shattered with precise disorder,
An eggshell yacht aground in blues and greens.

Used to this fishing town
And unsurprised by what the wind unwraps
From fog, I wait for crevices of flashing blue
My rising apprehension
Or a sun-spiked seagull might get through
Until, by somersault of my good sense,
My upcast eyes downcast on roofs, sails, spars,
As if I were the first voyeur from Mars,
I go stark blind through long familiar lanes
Where dogs scratch, horses champ, and friends

Cut grass on week-days, Sundays wash their cars.
O when at noon a lightning-crooked seam
Opens the world to my world blazing down,
I wonder under heaven who I am.

Most real and most unknown,
Anarchic village, do not lead me on.
The house I live in painted weather-white,
The sprawl of fence-rose that I lean upon
Contain me and ingratiate me well
As four-square in my roots, and on my guard,
I watch sea-twilight bundle up the yard
And trick my town out like the Pleiades.
Yet my wild sleep's reversals find me caught:
Dead reckoning, I have long ago put out—
The sun I wake to folds another sun,
The moon I ride swings a still colder moon;
Patience, white village, I shall find you soon.